How to Draw...

Fantasy Creatures

Dragons, fairies, vampires & monsters in simple steps

MW00818157

First published in Great Britain 2015 by

Search Press Limited
Wellwood, North Farm Road,
Tunbridge Wells, Kent TN2 3DR

How to Draw Fantasy Creatures is a compendium volume of
illustrations taken from the How to Draw series:
How to Draw Dragons; How to Draw Fairies;
How to Draw Vampires and How to Draw Monsters.

ISBN: 978-1-78221-309-3

Printed in Malaysia

How to Draw
Fantasy
Creatures

Dragons, fairies, vampires & monsters in simple steps

Paul Bryn Davies & Jim McCarthy

Search Press

Contents

Introduction...8

Dragons...10

Page 12

Page 13

Page 14

Page 15

Page 16

Page 17

Page 18

Page 19

Page 20

Page 21

Page 22

Page 23

Page 24

Page 25

Page 26

Page 27

Page 28

Page 29

Page 30

Page 31

Page 32

Page 33

Page 34

Page 35

Page 36

Page 38

Fairies..40

Page 42

Page 43

Page 44

Page 45

Page 46

Page 47

Page 48

Page 49

Page 50

Page 51

Page 52

Page 53

Page 54

Page 55

Page 56

Page 57

Page 58

Page 59

Page 60

Page 61

Page 62

Page 63

Page 64

Page 65

Page 66

Page 67

Page 68

Page 69

Vampires..**70**

Page 72

Page 73

Page 74

Page 75

Page 76

Page 77

Page 78

Page 79

Page 80

Page 81

Page 82

Page 83

Page 84

Page 85

Page 86

Page 87

Page 88

Page 89

Page 90

Page 91

Page 92

Page 93

Page 94

Page 96

Page 97

Monsters...98

Page 100

Page 101

Page 102

Page 103

Page 104

Page 105

Page 106

Page 107

Page 108

Page 109

Page 110

Page 111

Page 112

Page 113

Page 114

Page 115

Page 116

Page 117

Page 118

Page 119

Page 120

Page 121

Page 122

Page 123

Page 124

Page 125

Page 126

Page 127

Introduction

Artists Paul Bryn Davies and Jim McCarthy are experts in drawing the wierd and wonderful. This step-by-step collection of their sketches provides you with an exciting range of fun and fictitious characters to draw.

These drawings are designed to inspire and will act as a starting point to help you to capture their unique creative flair. The method of illustration is simple: basic geometric shapes evolve, stage by stage, into the finished forms. In order to make the sequences easier to follow, the artists use different coloured pencils for each of the stages. The colours act as a guide, with new shapes built on to old shapes, and distinguishing features are added as the images develop. The penultimate stages show tonal representations of the fantasy creatures, and the final stage is a full colour image of the finished drawing.

When you are following the steps, use an HB, B or 2B pencil. Draw lightly, so that any intial, unwanted lines can be erased easily. Your final work could be a detailed pencil drawing, or the pencil lines can be drawn over using a ballpoint, felt-tip or technical pen. At this point, gently erase the original pencil lines.

If you want to add colour, you could use pencil crayons, markers, watercolours or acrylics. Alternatively, if you have the equipment and the skills, your drawings can be scanned into a computer and coloured digitally. Watercolours have been applied using an airbrush and opaque white gouache has been added as highlights.

Once you get the hang of it, you may want to try drawing your own fantasy creations; perhaps from your own photographs, using the simple construction method shown here. You can make the process easier if you use tracing paper to transfer shapes and lines to your drawing.

Most importantly, remember to have fun drawing these imaginative (and sometimes terrifying) creatures!

Happy drawing!

Dragons

Here, you will learn how to create the greatest of all mythical beasts: the dragon. These legendary creatures come in a selection of different styles, from fierce, fire-breathing beasts to friendly, crouching and sleeping dragons.

To create your own compositions, it is a good idea to look at crocodiles, iguanas, lizards and other reptiles for inspiration.

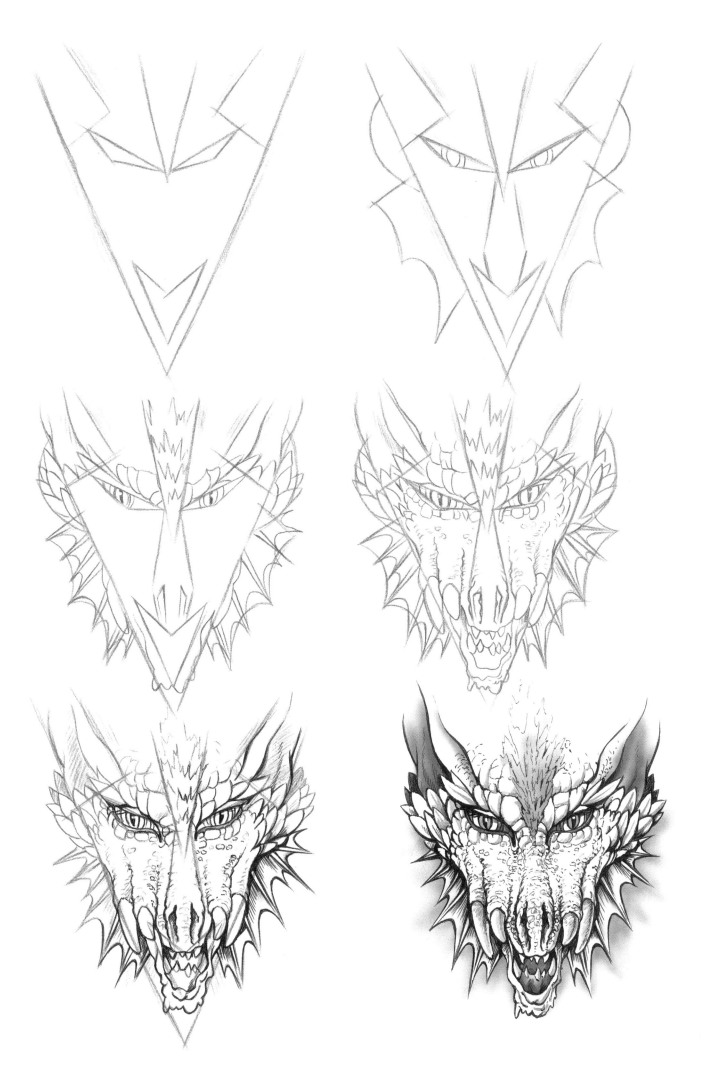

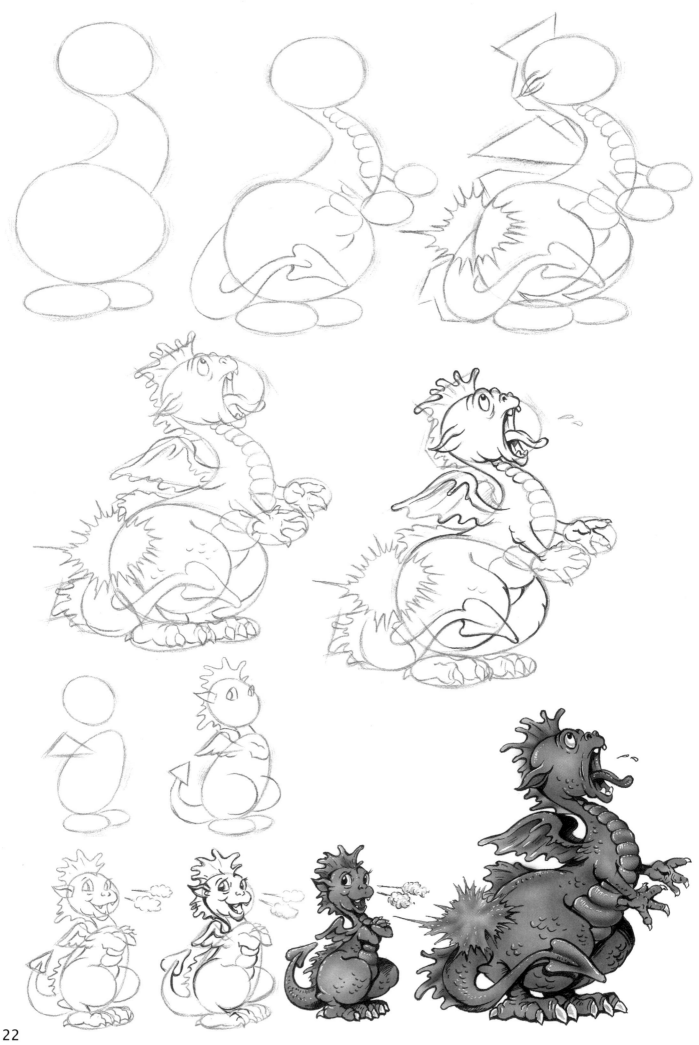

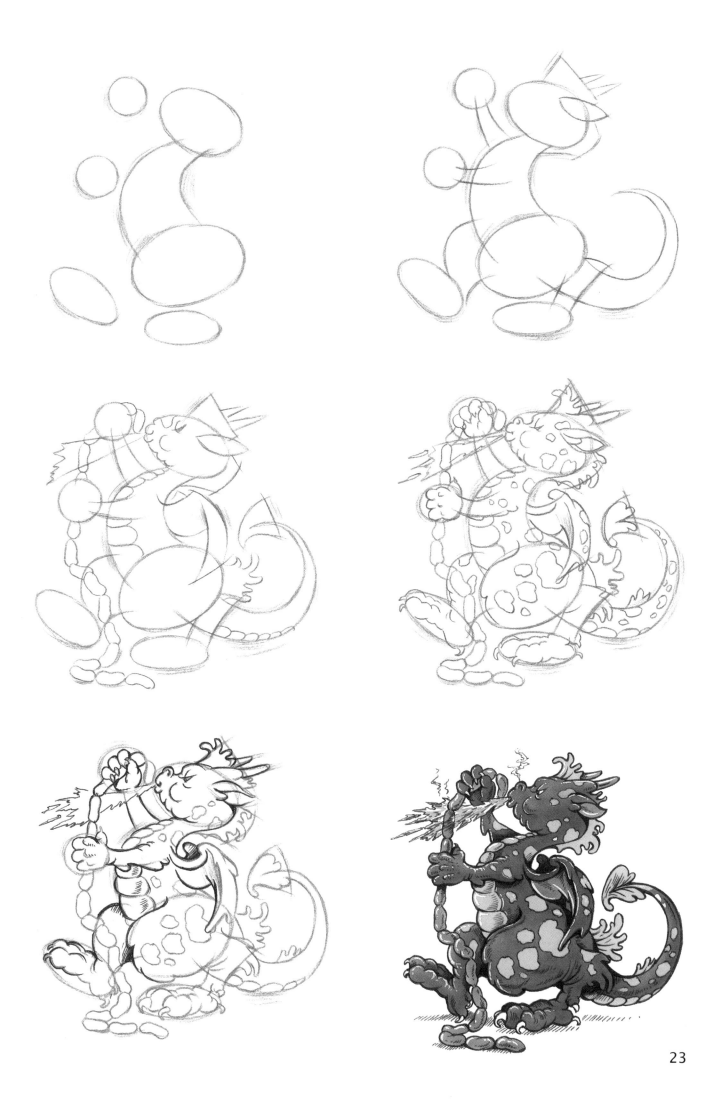

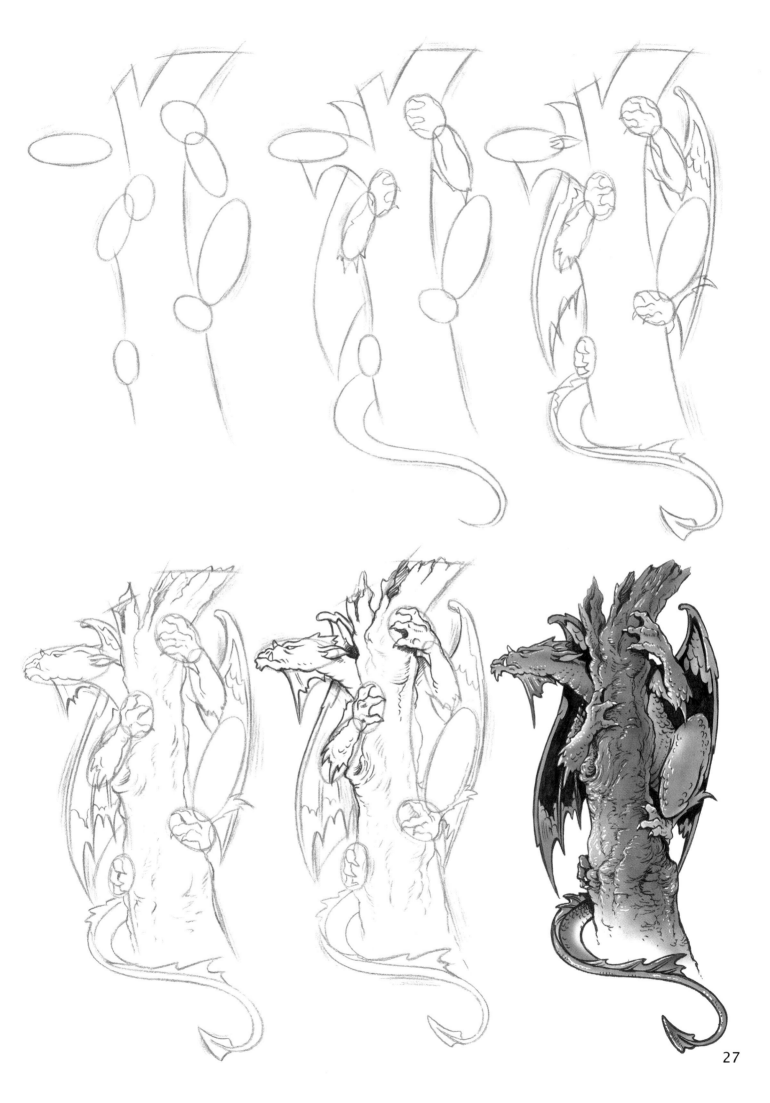

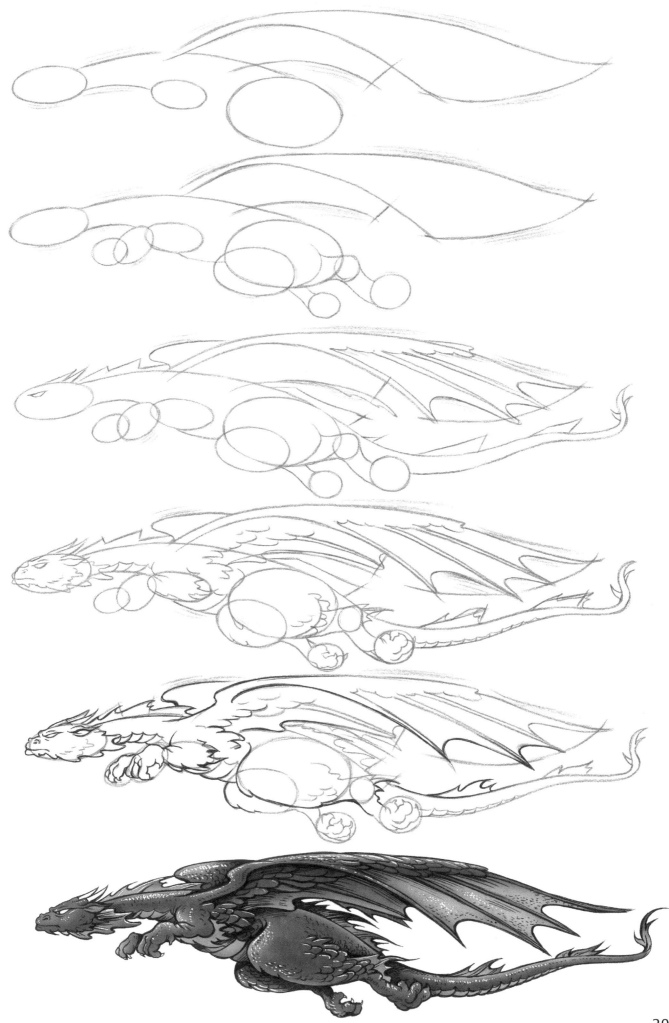

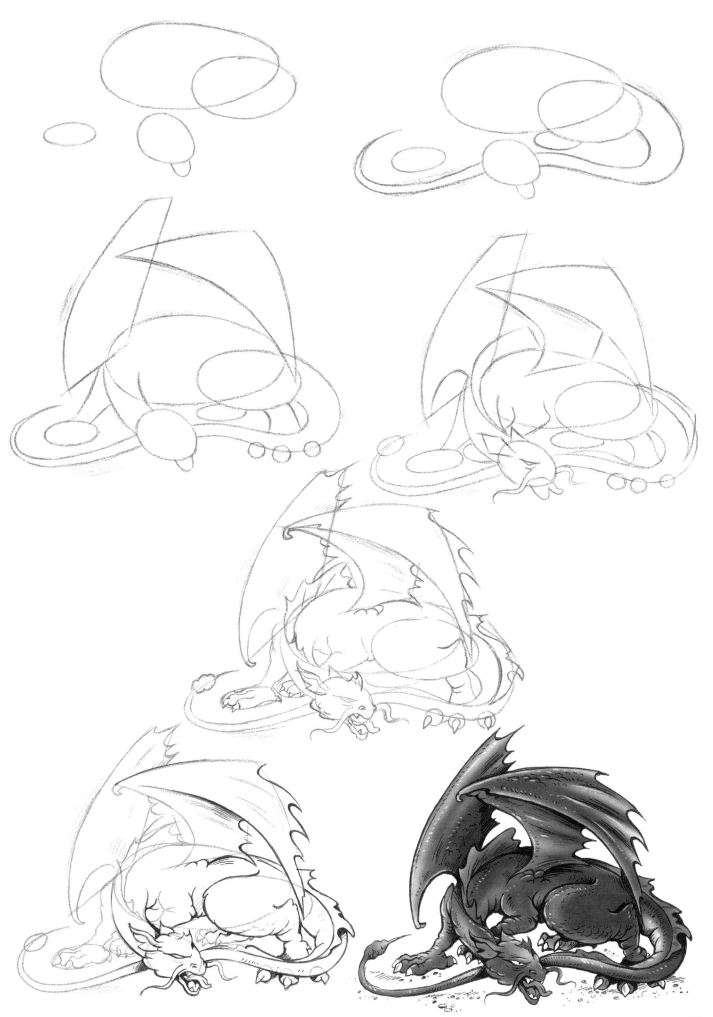

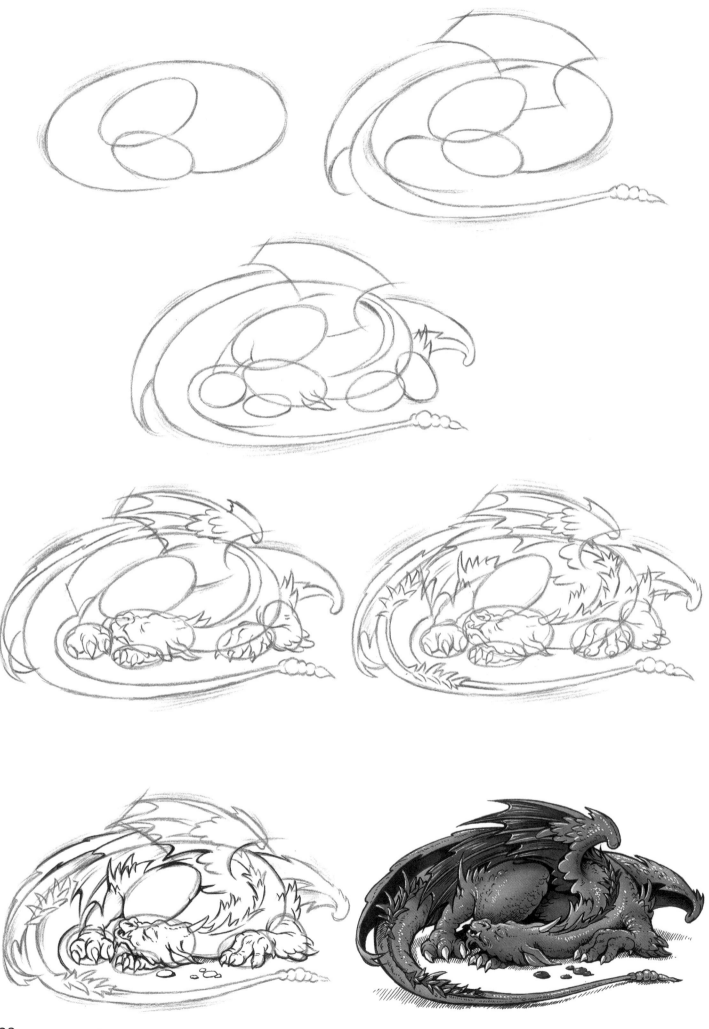

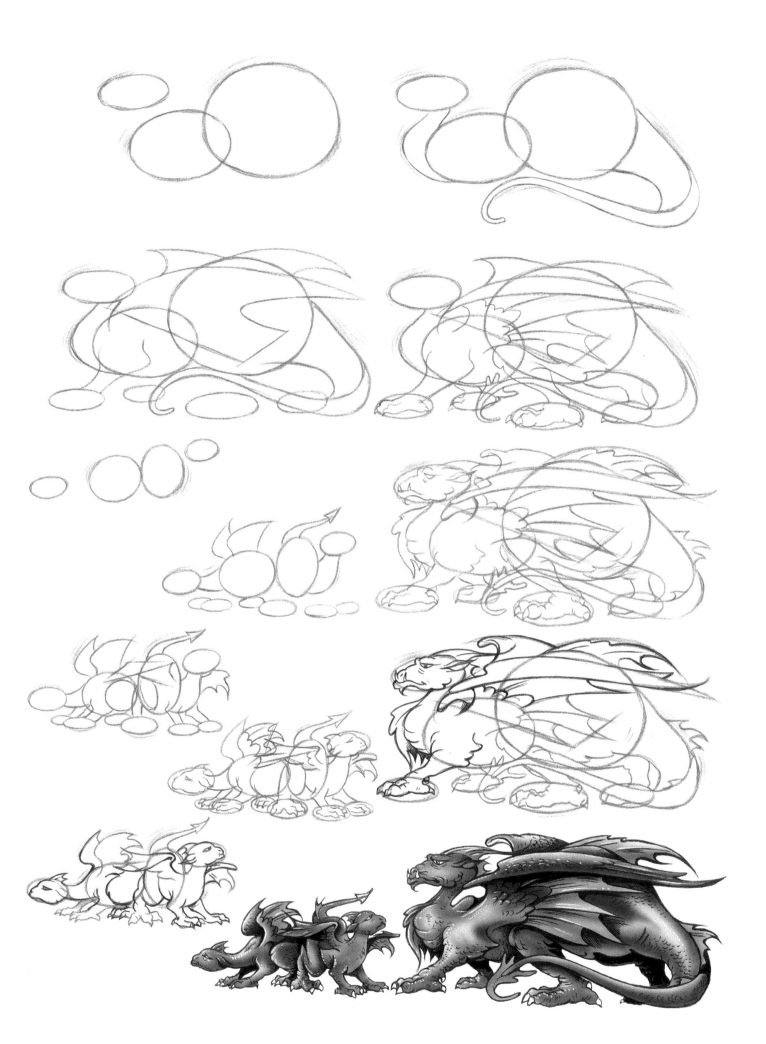

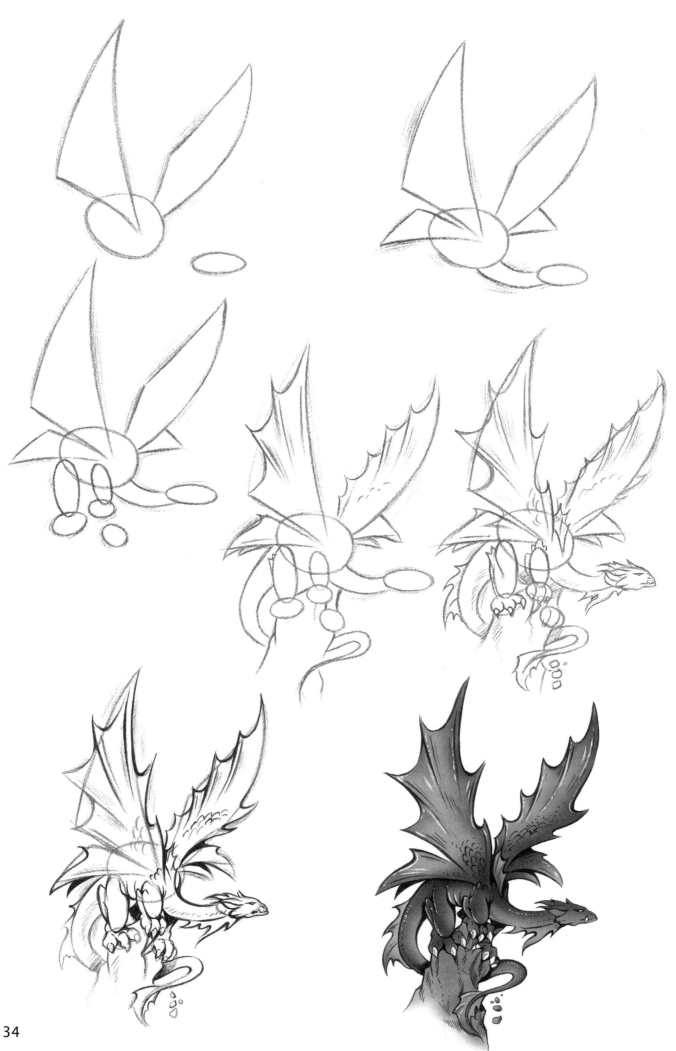

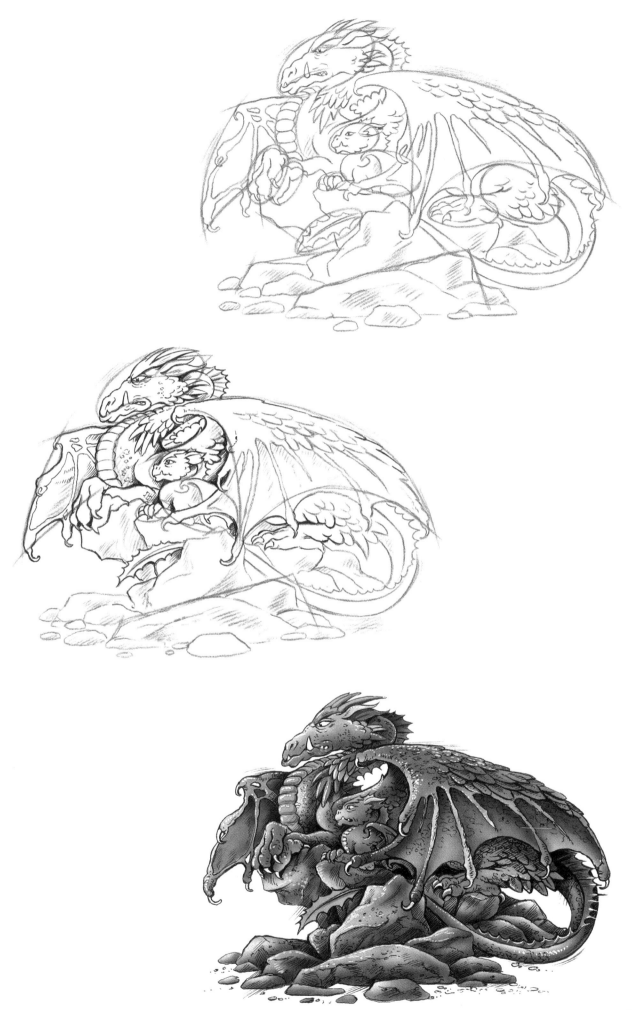

Fairies

Welcome to Fairyland! Paul Bryn Davies has provided a varied collection from cartoon-style winged folk to more realistic fairies; some mischievous, others beguiling, but all of them beautiful.

If you believe in the legends about these elusive creatures, you will know that they are impossible to find, so inspiration must be taken from nature as well as rural and urban environments. Fairies closely resemble humans and understanding the basics of human anatomy will help if you want to progress and draw your own folk. When drawing the wings, try studying the wings of butterflies, lacewings and similar flying insects.

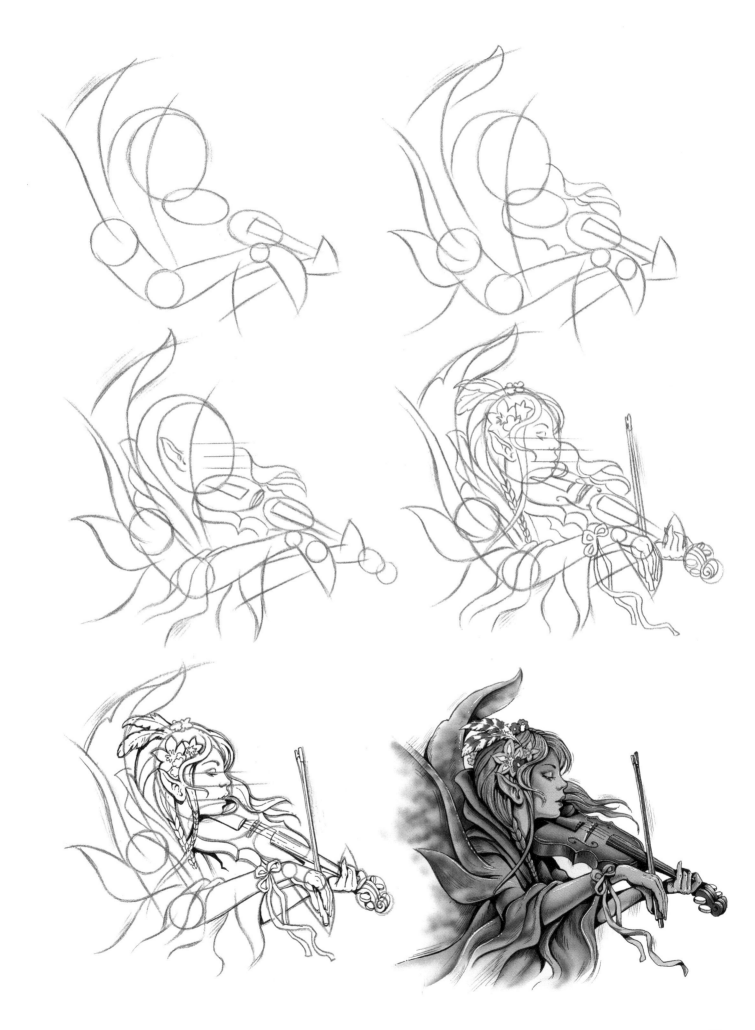

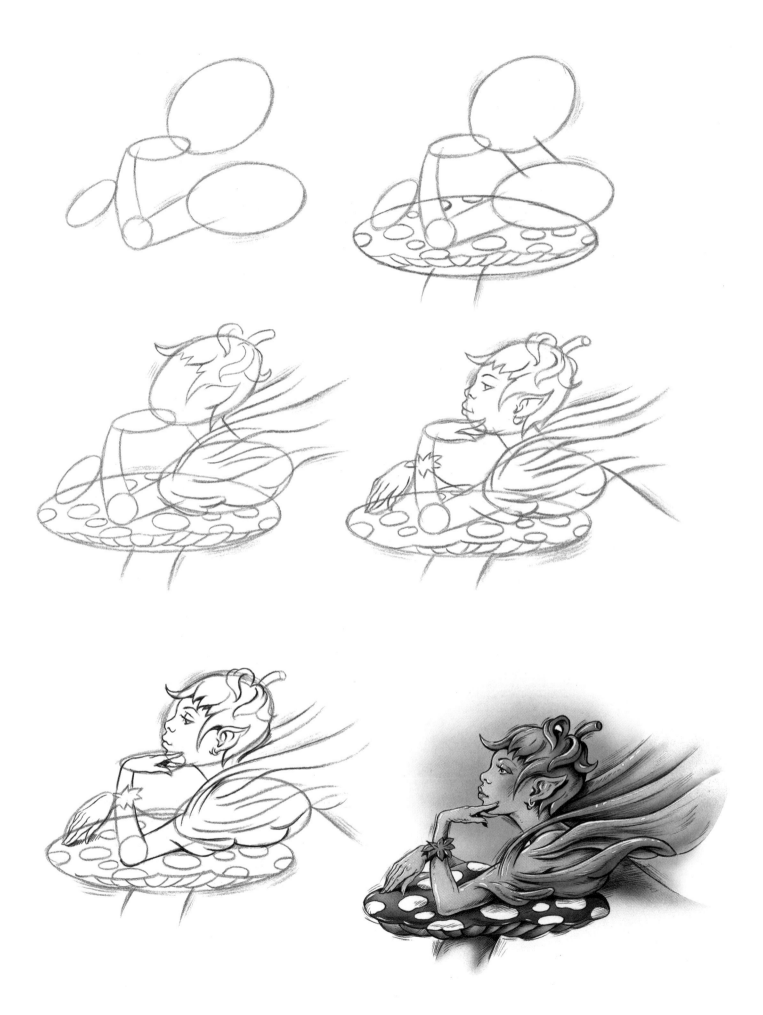

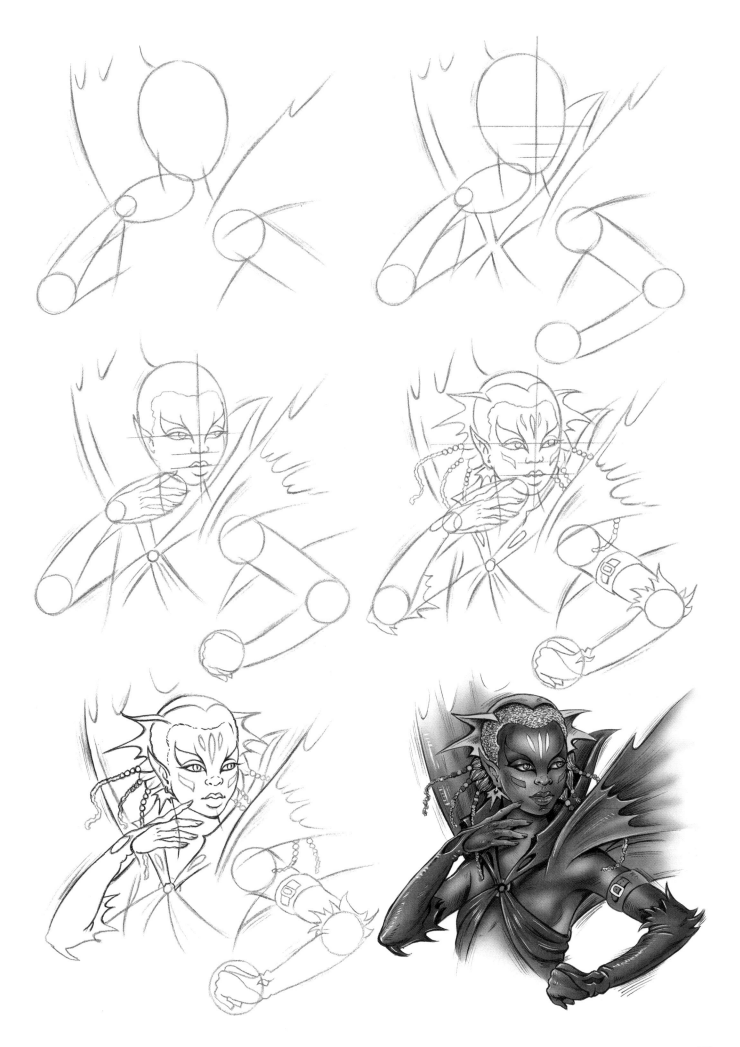

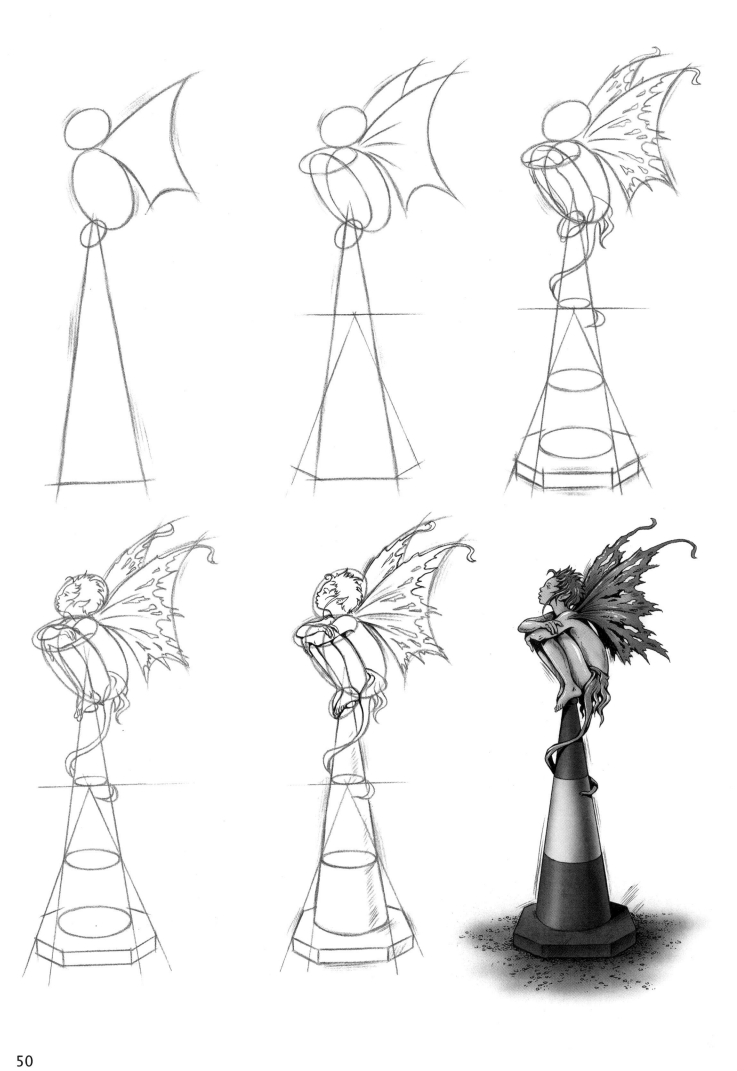

53

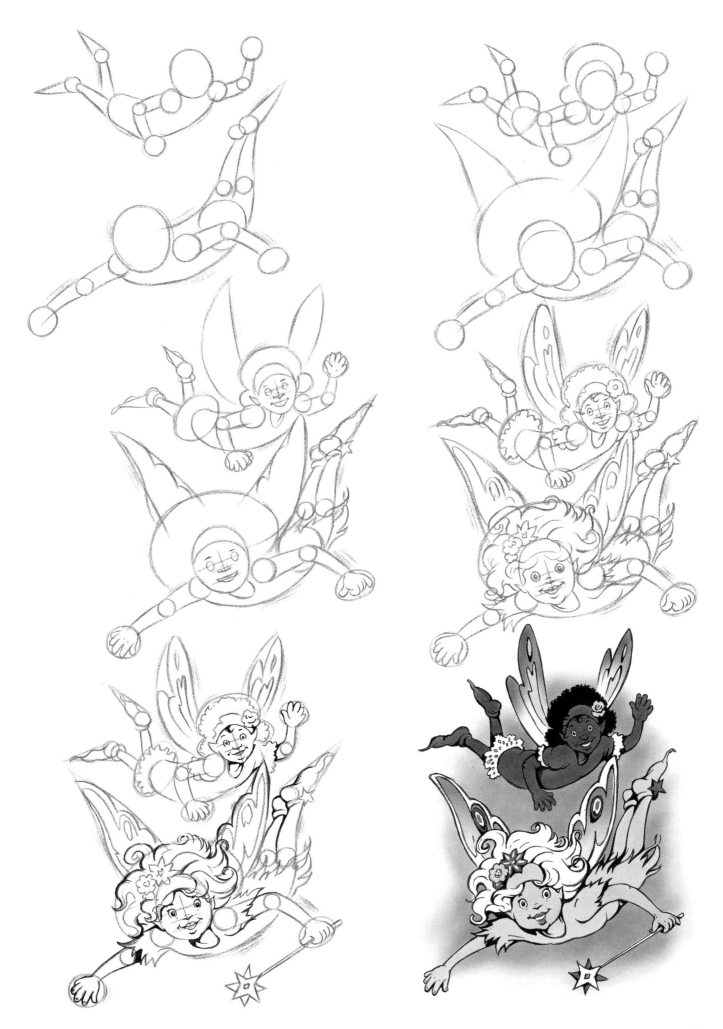

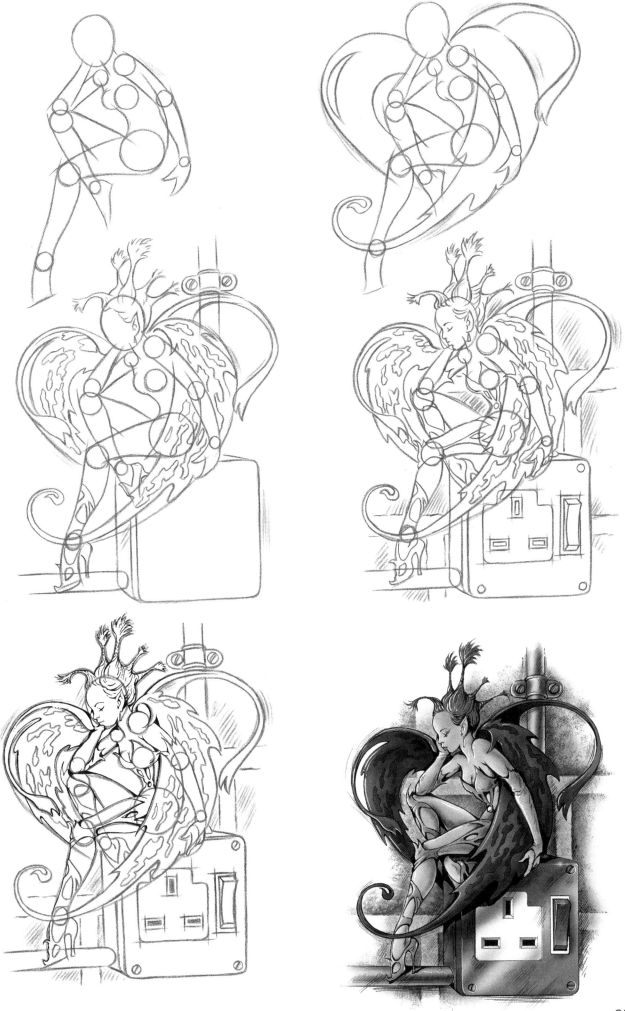

66

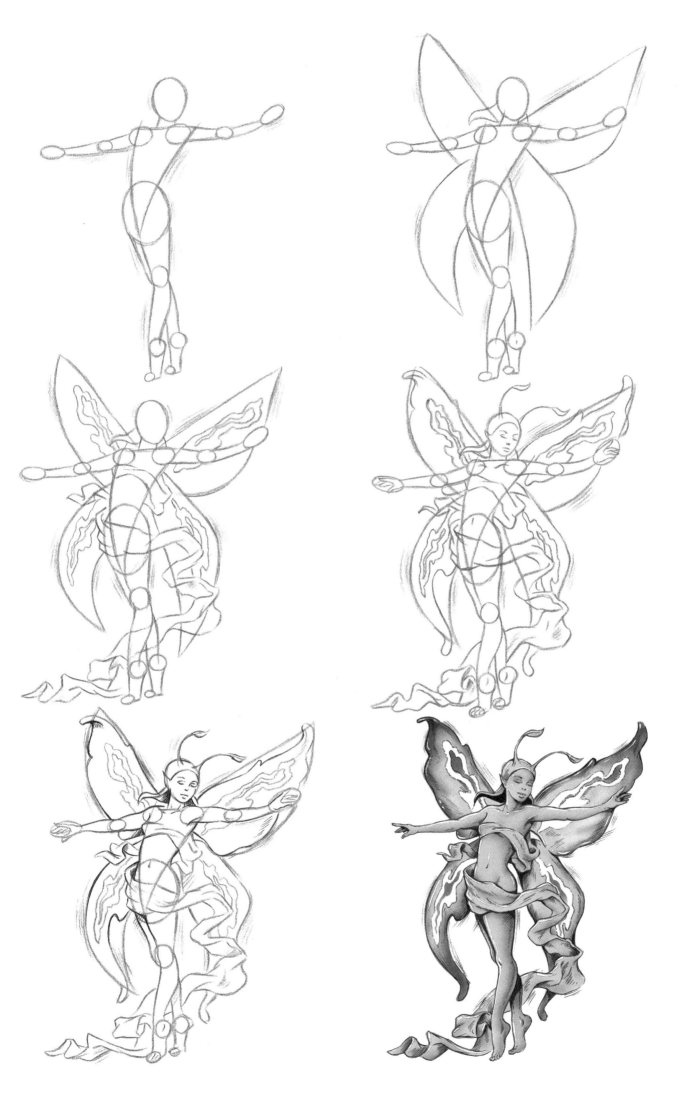

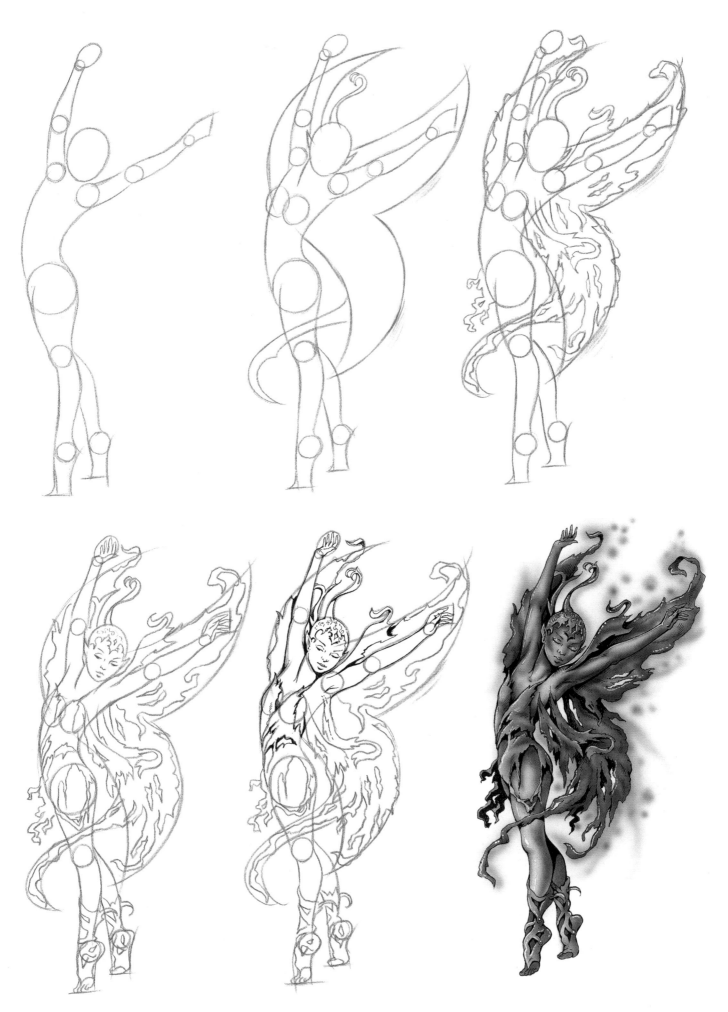

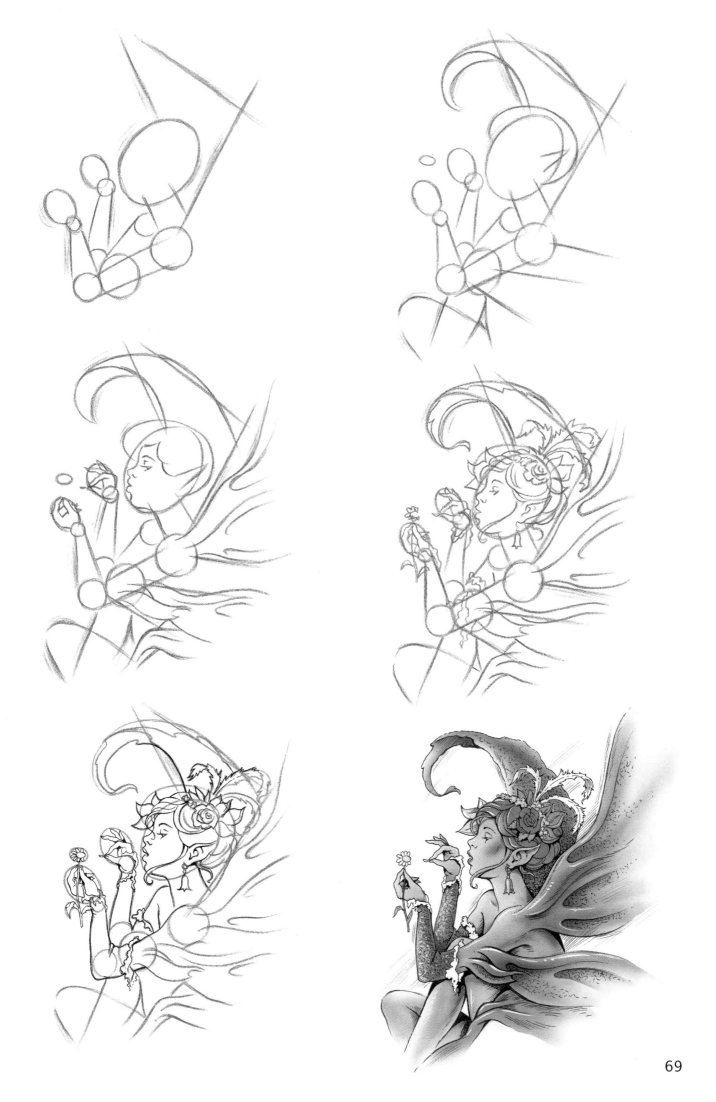

Vampires

Welcome to nightfall – when the vampires rise to drink! This selection includes a broad range of frightening and sometimes beautiful vampires in different styles, both male and female. Some feature a menacing atmosphere with bats, tombstones and castles as part of the backdrop. This type of setting can enhance a character considerably and it does not have to be complicated.

Understanding the basics of human anatomy will really help you to create your own vampires. It is a good idea to look at photographic reference for the basic figure. Magazines, mail order catalogues or photographs of family and friends are a great source of inspiration – though, hopefully, not for the fang-like teeth! An artist's mannequin is also useful for creating the foundation of your vampire drawing. Seek inspiration for clothing by looking at costumes, both old and new.

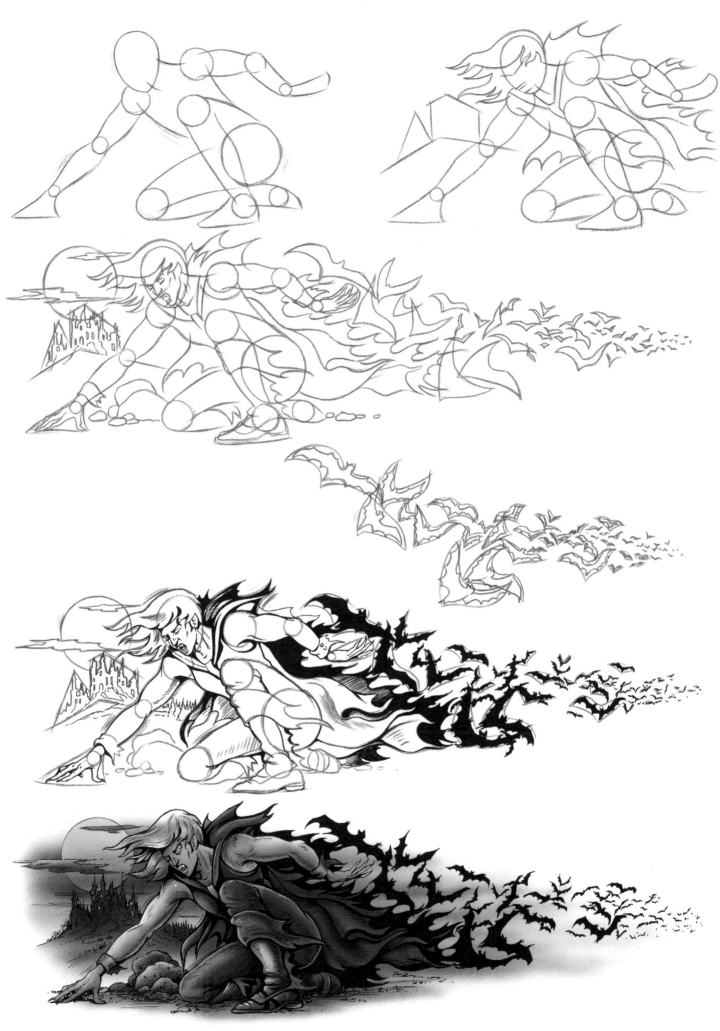

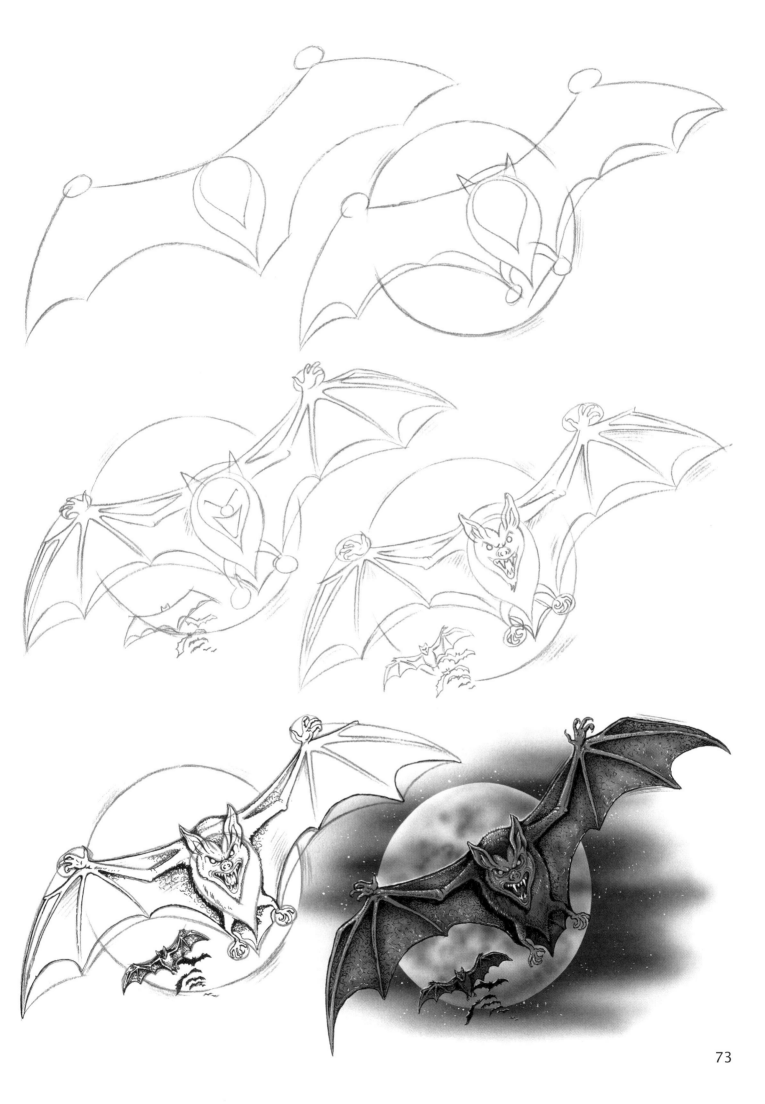

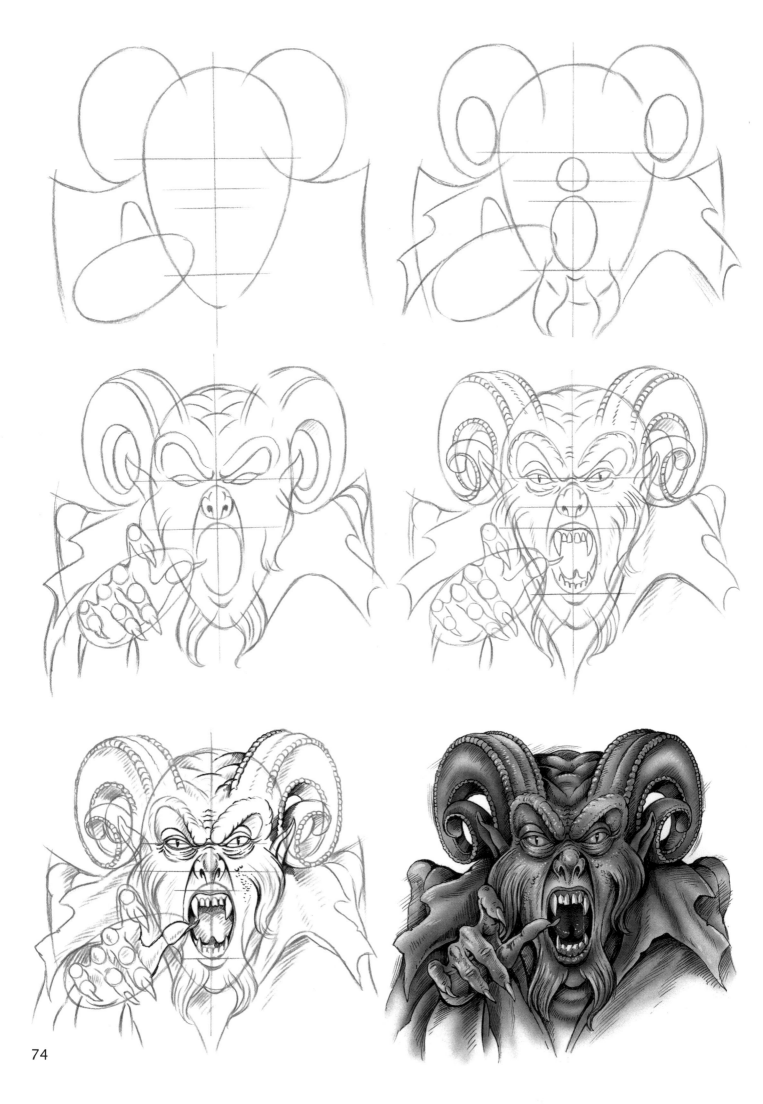

74

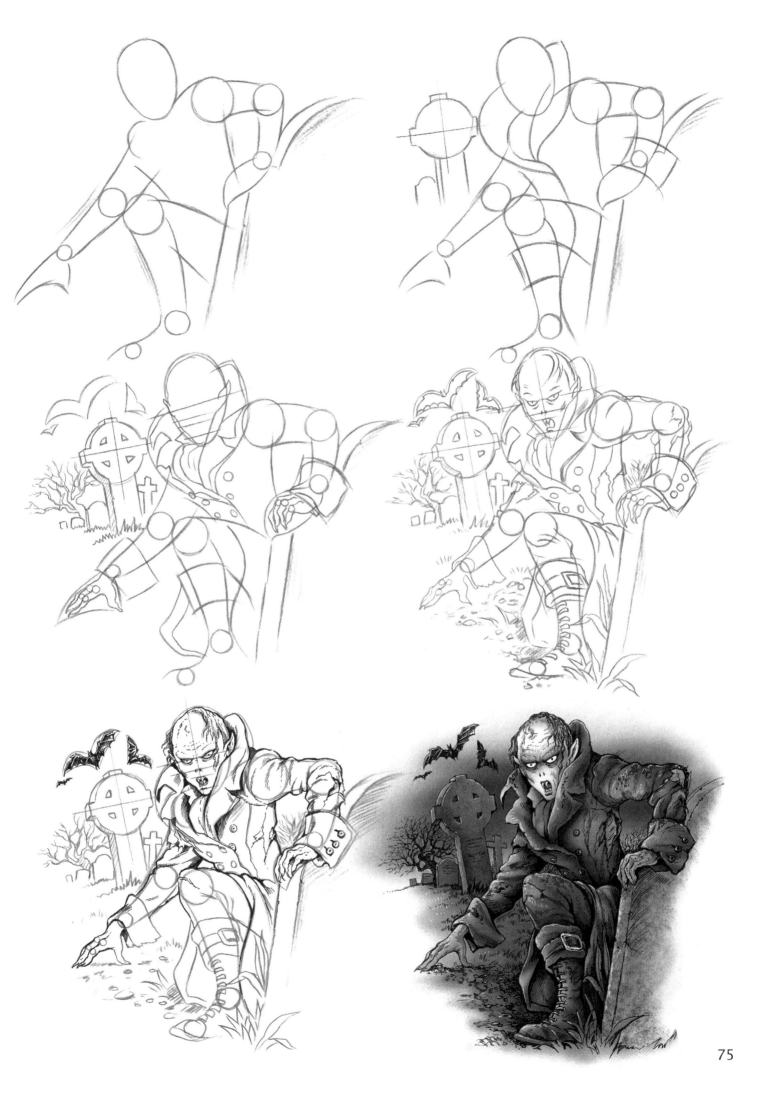

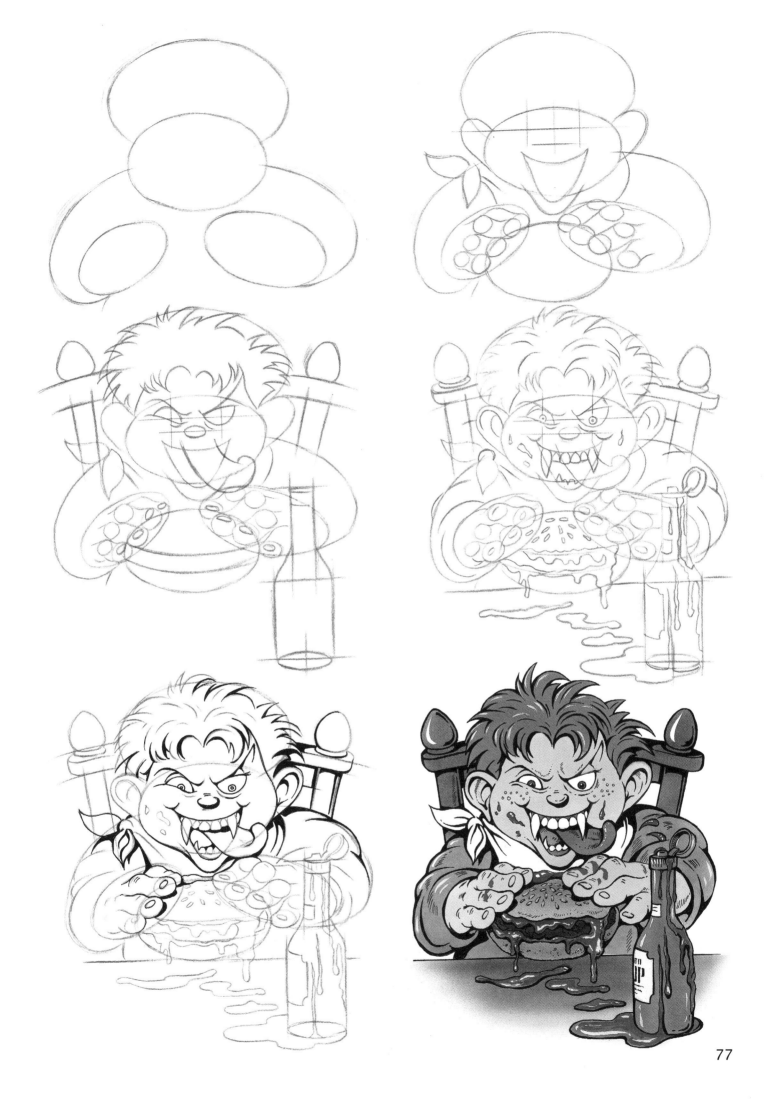

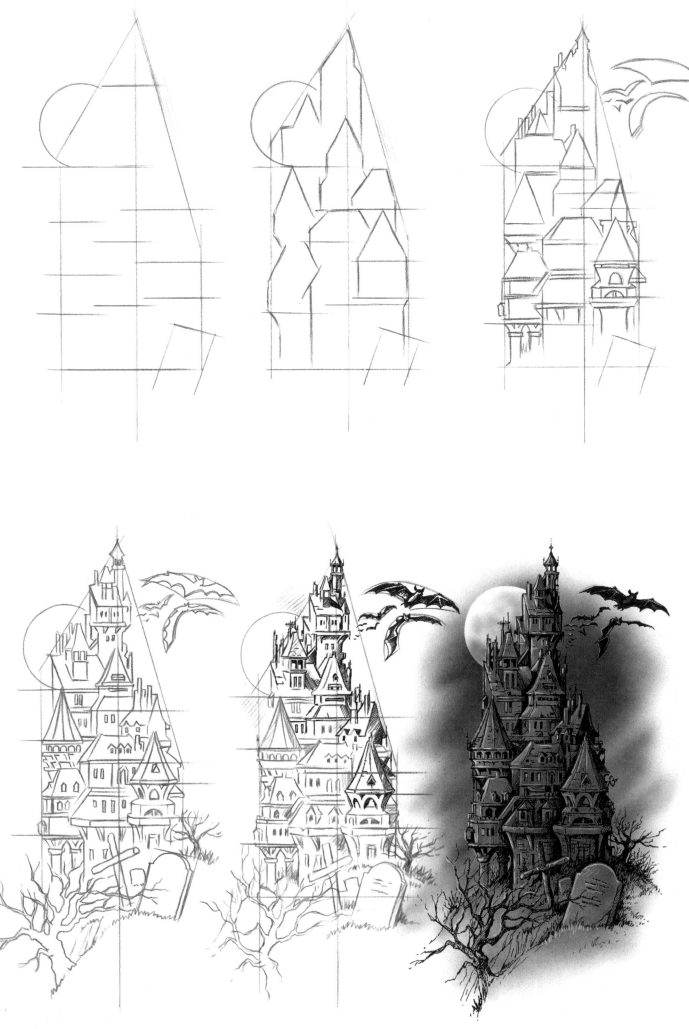

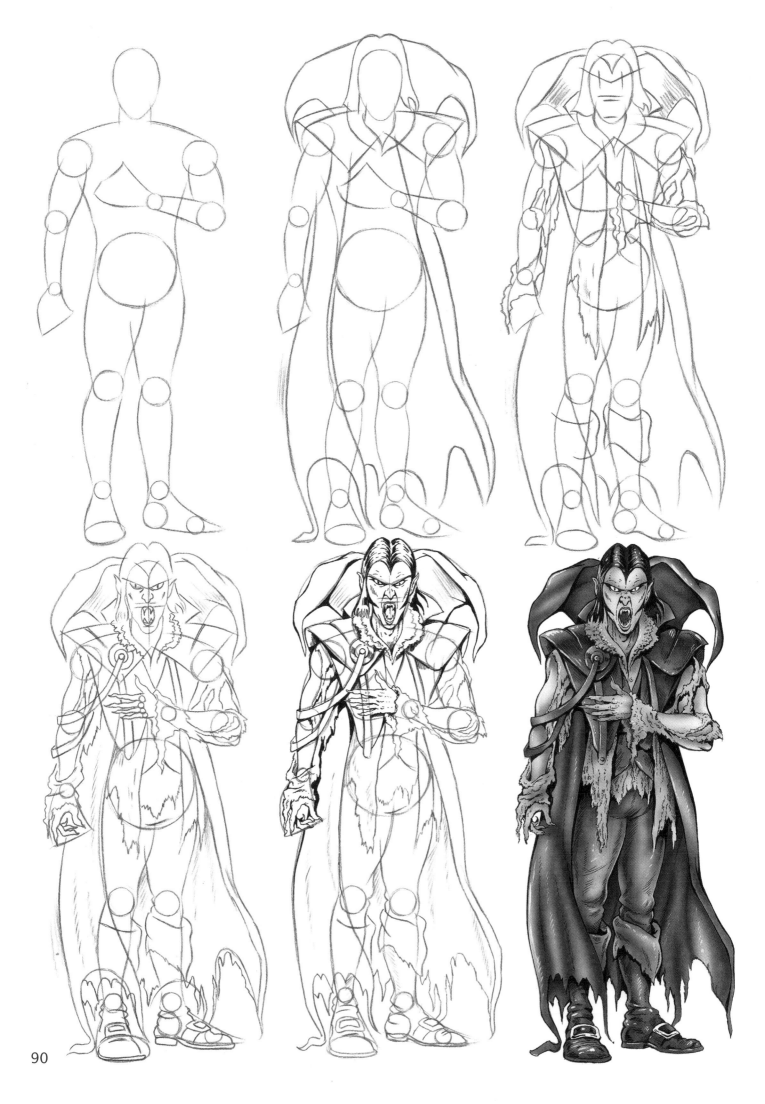

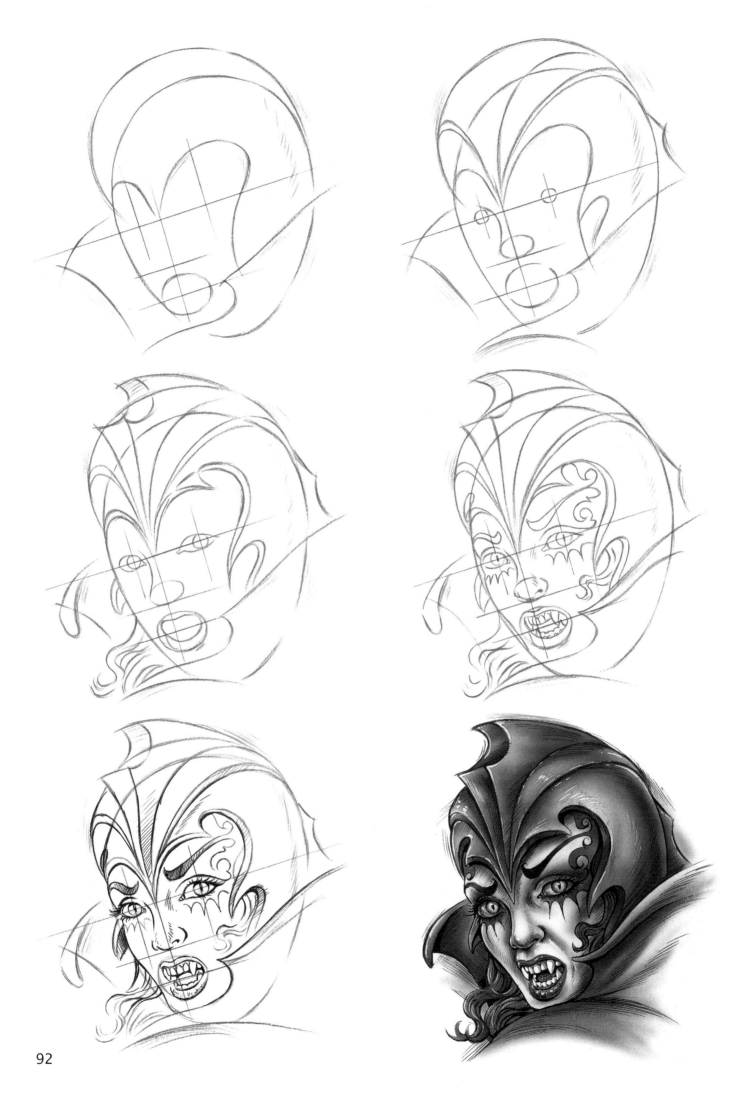

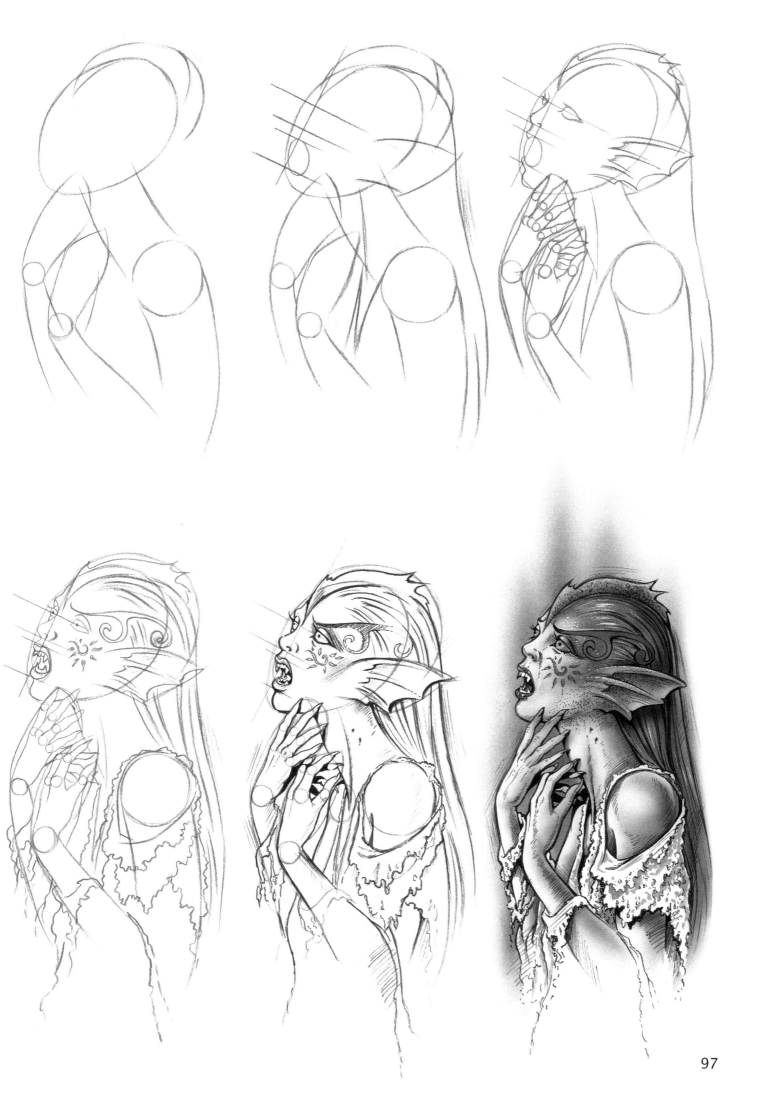

Monsters

Monsters can be scary, funky and even downright cool. There are just so many ways to draw these fun characters – you can make them cute, angry, ghostly or just plain grotesque!

When creating your own characters, remember it's all about adding monstrous features, so don't forget the fangs, big teeth, hairy tufts, strange eyeballs, menacing faces and ghoulish expressions.

100

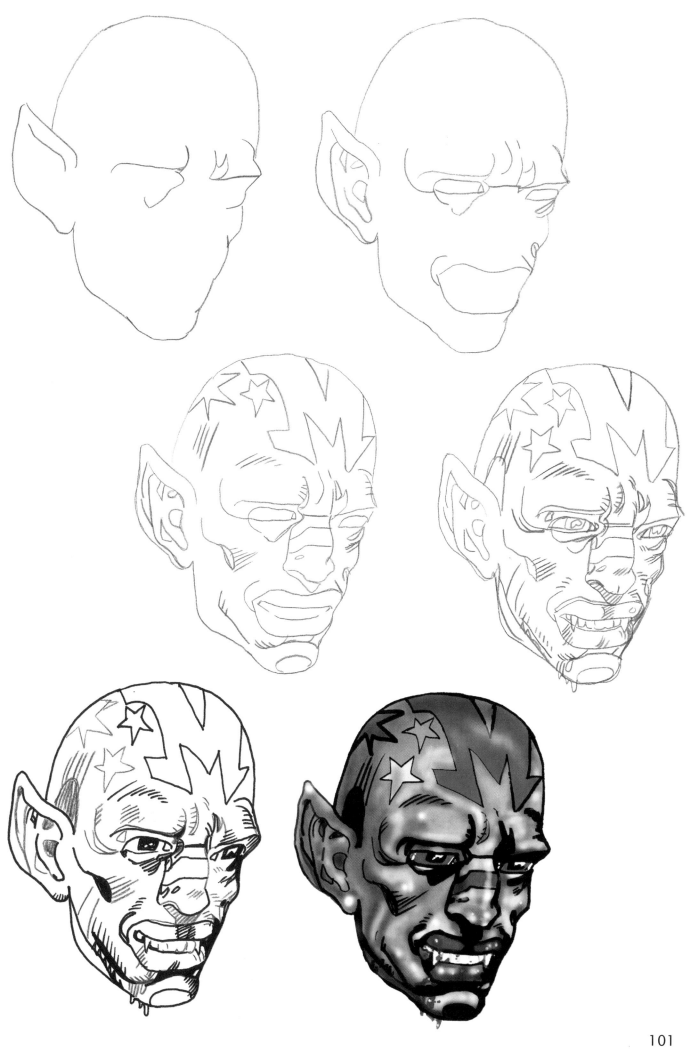

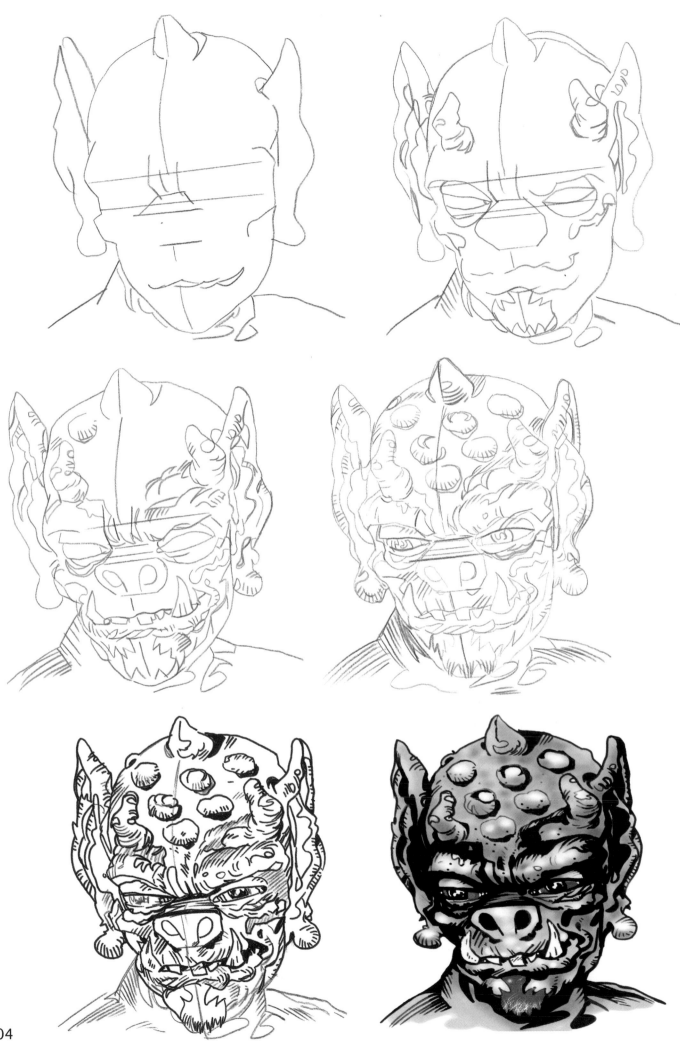

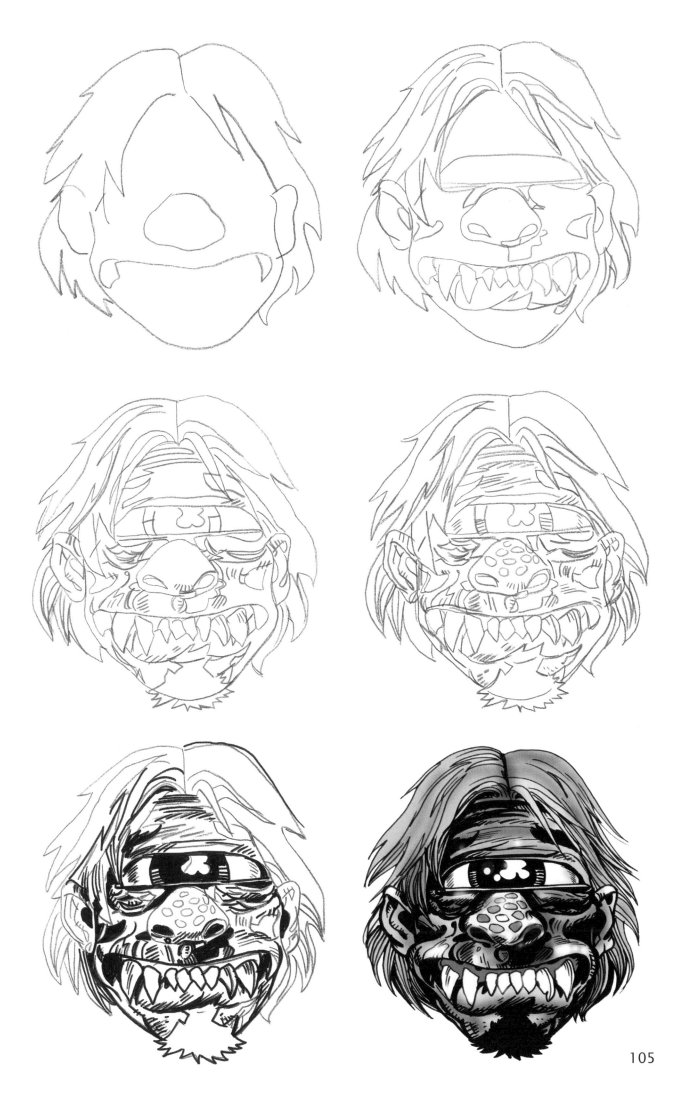

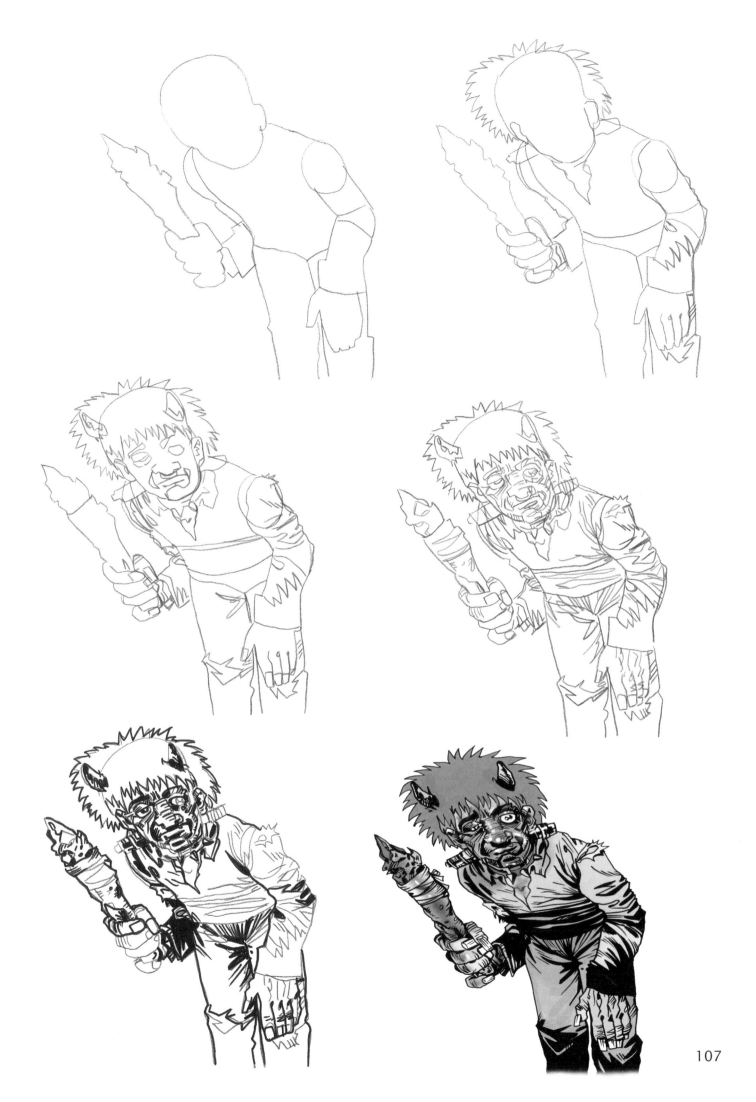

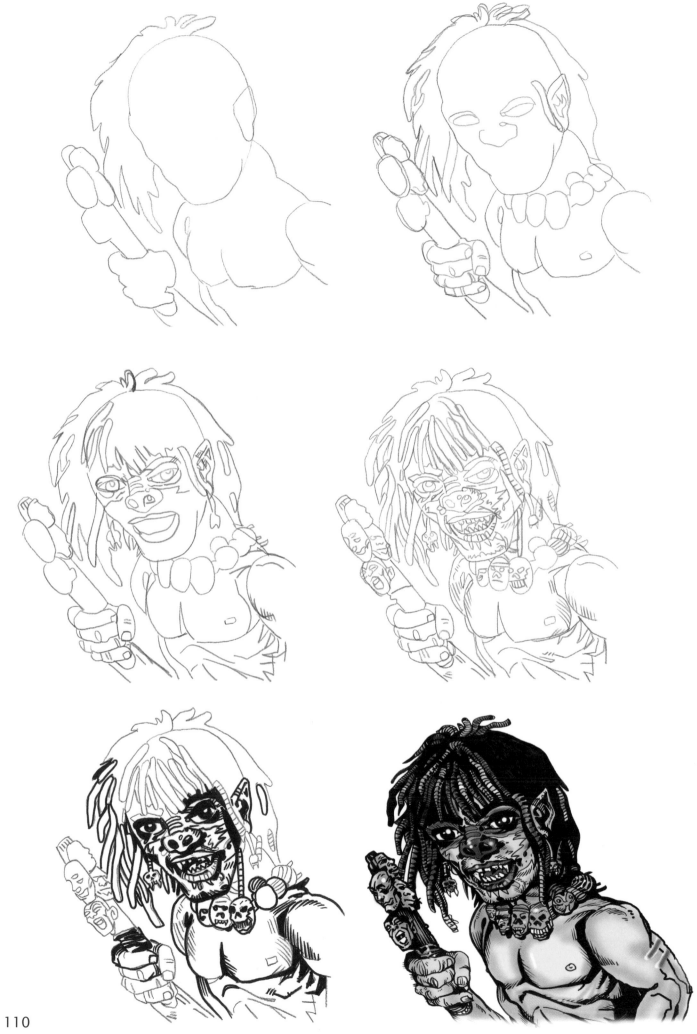

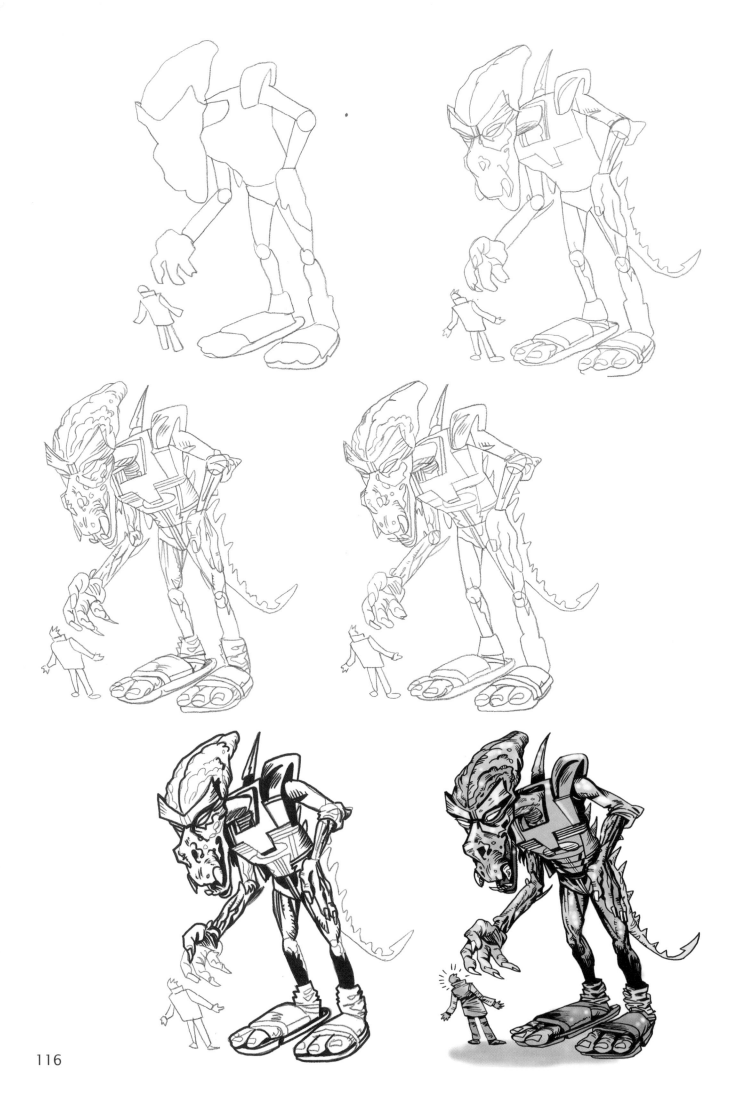

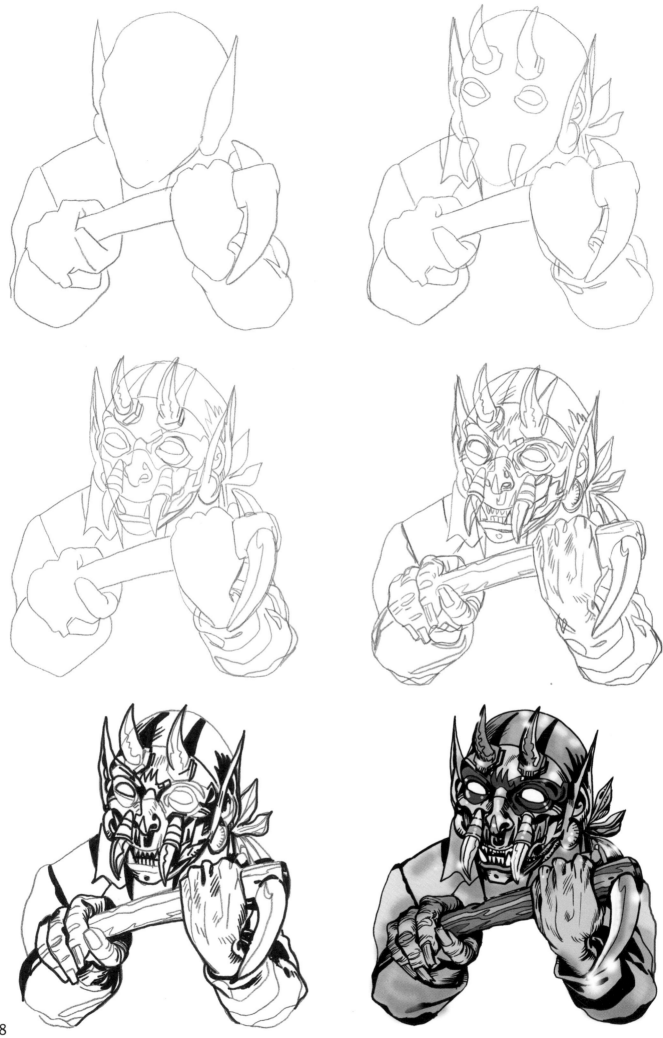

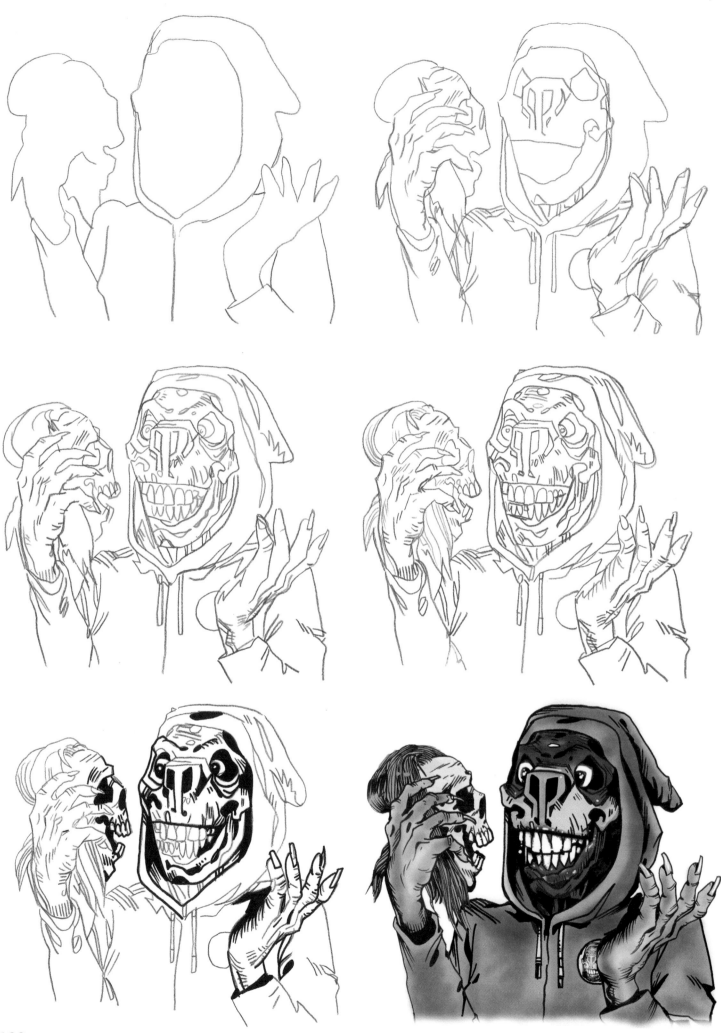

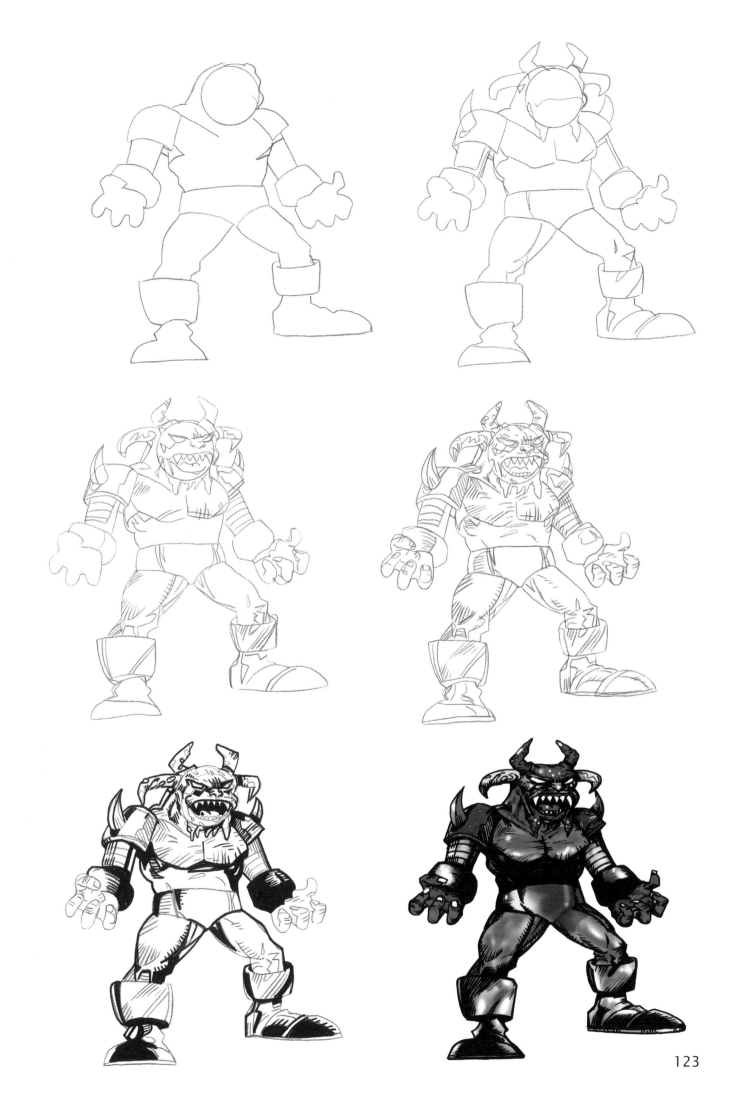

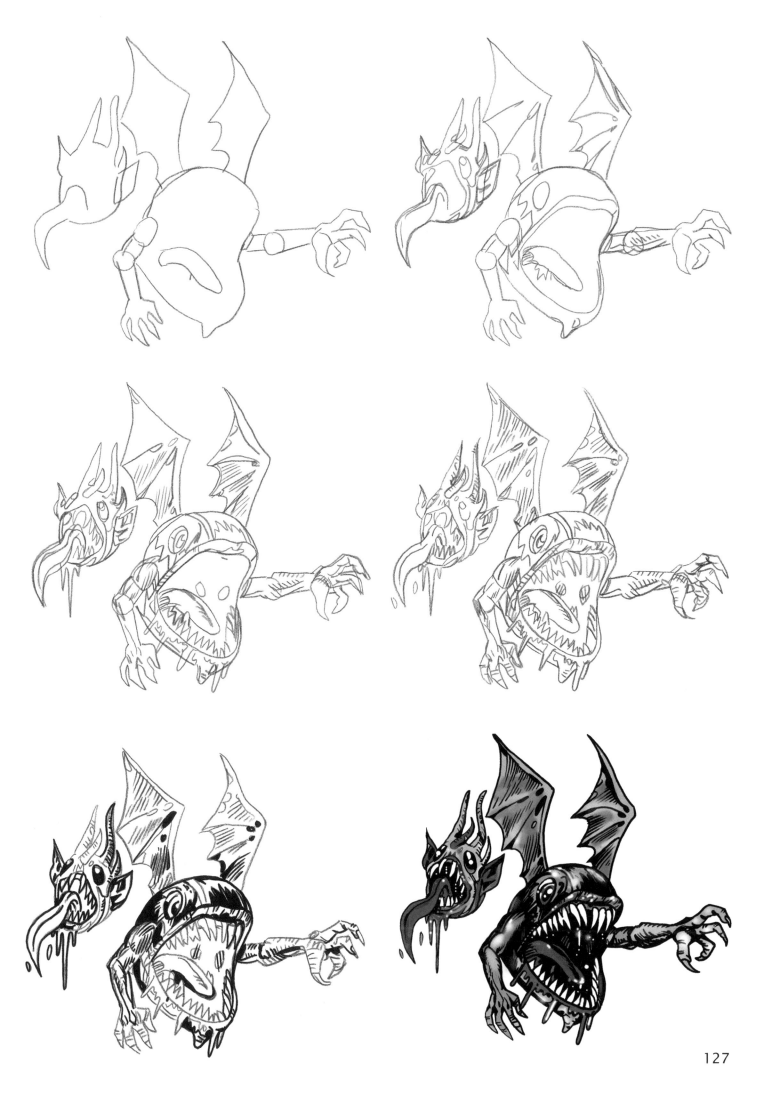